WILLARD LEROY METCALF

W. L. Metcalf, c. 1885,
courtesy of Mr. Addison Metcalf

WILLARD LEROY METCALF

A Retrospective

SELECTION *&* CATALOGUE BY FRANCIS MURPHY

WITH A BIOGRAPHICAL ESSAY BY ELIZABETH DEVEER

ORGANIZED BY THE MUSEUM OF FINE ARTS · SPRINGFIELD

SUPPORTED BY THE NATIONAL ENDOWMENT FOR THE ARTS

MUNSON-WILLIAMS-PROCTOR INSTITUTE · UTICA
SEPTEMBER 5 · OCTOBER 10 · 1976

MUSEUM OF FINE ARTS · SPRINGFIELD
OCTOBER 24 · DECEMBER 26 · 1976

THE CURRIER GALLERY OF ART · MANCHESTER
JANUARY 14 · MARCH 6 · 1977

HUNTER MUSEUM OF ART · CHATTANOOGA
APRIL 3 · MAY 15 · 1977

FOREWORD

Mr. Budd H. Bishop, Director of the Hunter Museum of Art in Chattanooga, Tennessee; Mr. David S. Brooke, Director of The Currier Gallery of Art in Manchester, New Hampshire; and Mr. Edward H. Dwight, Director of the Munson-Williams-Proctor Institute in Utica, New York, join me in expressing appreciation to the National Endowment for the Arts for their generous financial support of this exhibition. Visitors to the exhibition and readers of this catalogue will certainly agree with us that this is an important return to them of a portion of their tax dollar. The beauty alone of Metcalf's art would justify such an expenditure; the scholarship and permanent record that this publication represents speak further for the soundness of the Endowment's assistance program.

Professor Francis Murphy has worked assiduously and with unflagging spirit on this exhibition. We heartily thank him. Dr. Murphy's enthusiasm for American art and brilliance as one of New England's leading cognoscenti are wedded to his own professional expertise in American literature in the pages of this catalogue. It will serve, I believe, as a model for the humanistic treatment of the history of art and will also be of lasting value in bringing enlightenment and attention to the lovely images of Willard Leroy Metcalf.

Richard C. Mühlberger, *Director*
Museum of Fine Arts
Springfield, Massachusetts

February, 1976

LENDERS TO THE EXHIBITION

AKRON ART INSTITUTE, AKRON, OHIO

ALBRIGHT-KNOX ART GALLERY, BUFFALO, NEW YORK

ANONYMOUS LENDERS

THE ART INSTITUTE OF CHICAGO, CHICAGO, ILLINOIS

MR. AND MRS. FRED D. BENTLEY, SR., AND MR. AND MRS. J. ALAN SELLARS

BERRY-HILL GALLERIES, NEW YORK, NEW YORK

THE BROOKLYN MUSEUM, BROOKLYN, NEW YORK

CHAPELLIER GALLERIES, INC., NEW YORK, NEW YORK

COE KERR GALLERY, INC., NEW YORK, NEW YORK

CORCORAN GALLERY OF ART, WASHINGTON, D.C.

THE CURRIER GALLERY OF ART, MANCHESTER, NEW HAMPSHIRE

MR. AND MRS. COLIN M. CURTIS

DALLAS MUSEUM OF FINE ARTS, DALLAS, TEXAS

DAVIS AND LONG COMPANY, NEW YORK, NEW YORK

THE DENVER ART MUSEUM, DENVER, COLORADO

MR. AND MRS. PAUL FELTMAN

MRS. F. BAILEY HALL

INTRODUCTION

EVEN GRANTING the vagaries of modern taste, the virtual disappearance of the name of Willard Metcalf from the history of modern American painting is a puzzling fact. The subject of considerable attention during his lifetime and the recipient of numerous awards and honors, Metcalf's name had sunk without trace ten years after his death. Oliver Larkin, in his influential *Art and Life in America* (1949), dismissed Metcalf as one more departed member of the "brood of Monet" who left behind him a legacy of saccharin landscapes, entirely lacking in Hassam's "vitality." Larkin chose *May Night* (1906) as a representative example of Metcalf's superficial theatricality: "the pale glimmering colonnade, the drifting figure are of the theatre, and like the theatre's effects they hold the interest only for a moment." While there are many things about this sentence with which one might argue, one could concede that *May Night* is one of Metcalf's more unguardedly romantic paintings. What Larkin and almost every historian who followed him did not acknowledge, undoubtedly because by the time they undertook their studies Metcalf's work had been relegated to the storage area or loaned out as decoration for the walls of charitable institutions, was that twenty more years' work followed and that Metcalf showed an extraordinary development in his art to the very end. No one today interested in American painting is unaware of the work of Theodore Robinson, J. Alden Weir, John Henry Twachtman, or, with the exception of Robert Reid and Edward Simmons, the rest of that group which referred to themselves as "The Ten." Metcalf remains anonymous. It is the primary purpose of this exhibition to present the first retrospective ever of this exemplary artist and to display his work to a viewing public, most of whom will be seeing his efforts for the first time in chronological order and in any number. I hope that there are enough examples included here to assure that Metcalf's mastery of the landscape will not be lost to yet another generation of students and collectors, and that he will take his rightful place among those American painters and poets who have engaged in what Wallace Stevens has called "the essential exercise"— the contemplation of the changing seasons with a full recognition that "there is nothing in the world greater than reality. In this predicament we have to accept reality itself as the only genius."

Metcalf acquired technical competence at an early age. Paintings included in this exhibition done before he was twenty provide ample evidence that he knew early on how to draw and handle paint with a natural gift which promised future growth. One has the sense, in fact, that all this may have come to him too easily. Until he was in his forties he cannot be said to have acquired a style of his own. In a painting like *Sandy Hollow* (1877) one is struck with parallels to William Merritt Chase; in the years in France he seems too close to Theodore Robinson for comfort, although the placement of the figures and draughtsmanship of *Turkeys in a Field* (c. 1886) is unmistakably Metcalf's. Robinson's influence continues well into the 1890's, and in the work Metcalf did at Gloucester Harbor (there is a well-known pastel which it was not possible to include in this exhibition) it was a happy one, but still, something of the personal element is missing. After 1900 the presence of J. Francis Murphy has to be accounted for in Metcalf's work, especially in paintings like *First Snow* (1906) or even *March Thaw* (1922). Both artists were represented by The Milch Gallery, but Murphy was a painter whose images were assimilated by Metcalf without dominating him in the way that Robinson's compositions and Twachtman's style might.

Royal Cortissoz, in his American Academy tribute to Metcalf, observed that "if ever a man had the principle of growth in him it was Metcalf." Beginning in 1903 Metcalf seems to have set out resolutely to find his own way with his art. As Mrs. de Veer notes, Metcalf referred to this as the start of his "renaissance." "He would leave the city," Cortissoz writes, "as for a campaign and bring back his sheaves with something of the air of a fighter who had conquered another step in his march." What Metcalf tackled, as a painting like *Afternoon Breeze* (1904) makes clear, was the problem of air

and light and color, and he did so in an impressionist manner which he avoided while in France, living in Giverny near the actual presence of Monet. Metcalf obviously never wanted to give himself over completely to color, to what Kermit Champa calls "total sensuousness of form." He respected drawing too much, he cared too much as a naturalist and an observer of the particular to move, like Monet, in the direction of abstraction. He hadn't read his *Walden* for nothing. *Pont Royal* (1913) and *Early Spring Afternoon* (1911) went about as far as Metcalf would ever go toward broken color. Perhaps he saw that once again in following that lead he would be competing with Hassam's pervasive examples. Metcalf was an impressionist only in the sense that he took his pleasures in the commonplace and the quotidian and that he saw the end of art as giving what Stevens called a "candid kind" to everything.

It is ironic that Metcalf's strength—his particularity—is the very thing which has been held against him. Richard Boyle in *American Impressionism* (1975) quotes approvingly the comment that Metcalf "did not deal in asperities" and leaves us with the feeling that Metcalf is the most prosaic of all his subjects, rather inclined toward illustration than art. Here again a quotation from Stevens' "Adagia" seems apt: "A grandiose subject is not an assurance of a grandiose effect but, most likely, of the opposite." Even in Metcalf's earliest landscapes—*Sandy Hollow* (1877) or *Diamond Island* (1879) —all inclinations toward the sublime as well as narrative have been resisted. Although he could draw the human figure ravishingly, the human element in relation to the landscape never interested him. What *did* interest him was what Stevens would call "weather"—the ambiance of air, light and shade, texture and color, the joy of experiencing the physical world. One keeps coming back to Stevens because, although twenty years Metcalf's junior, Stevens seems so parallel. They even *looked* alike. They both had a sensuous and bacchanalian side which they kept under careful control; both seemed to many acquaintances rather cold and forbidding; both seemed clumsy at personal relations; both admired elegance; but more important, they both spent their aesthetic lives exorcising the ghosts of Transcendentalists—all those asperities at which their intellectual fathers, Emerson and Thoreau, aimed at so intently. Metcalf is known to have been interested in spiritualism, but that has nothing to do with Transcendentalism. It says something about spiritualism that Metcalf took part in seances at the home of the realist Hamlin Garland. Spiritualists assume that people in the next world are intimately connected to this one. Their heaven is just an extension of reality. What Metcalf succeeded in doing was making images of the physical world that never strive toward "higher meaning." If his pictures "say" anything it is that the world without an Oversoul is a perfectly satisfying place to live and that human dignity consists in confronting a beautiful but alien Nature. That is why Metcalf's snow scenes are so compelling. At their best they succeed in conveying a slightly ominous sense of Nature at the same time that we are struck by its beauty. One thinks of some of the darker poems of Robert Frost, "The Most of It," for example, but it is Stevens' "The Snow Man" which presents the closest literary parallel to these moods, moments when we are aware of winter's particular beauty precisely because we have not added to it some purely human feeling, because we do not "think of any misery in the sound of the wind":

> Which is the sound of the land
> Full of the same wind
> That is blowing in the same bare place
>
> For the listener who listens in the snow
> And, nothing himself, beholds
> Nothing that is not there and the nothing that is.

In the last years of Metcalf's life he produced some of his most impressive works. He confronted the landscape of Chester, Vermont, and the Little Williams River, with a passion for recording its majesty and variety. His hand never seemed more sure, his eye never keener for the right detail or mass. No one can view these last pictures—and I have deliberately gathered together as many of them as I could—without respect for Metcalf as a painter. He may well have rejected "asperities." Like Frost, he knew that "The fact is the sweetest dream that labor knows."

The organization of a travelling exhibition the size of this one involves a great number of people. We are especially indebted to all those who generously lent their drawings and paintings and were willing to part with them for almost a year. Nothing would have been possible without their gracious loans. Mr. Jeffrey R. Brown, former Director of the Museum of Fine Arts, Springfield, first proposed this exhibition. Mr. Brown generously turned over to me his correspondence and notes and I turned to him frequently in the early stages of my work. Mrs. Elizabeth de Veer, who is at work on a catalogue raisonné and a biography of the artist, was kind enough to share her researches with me and to write a biographical sketch. Mr. Harold C. Milch, who continues at The Milch Gallery to be responsible for the frequent sale of Metcalf's work and is a mine of information about the painting and painters of this period, couldn't have been kinder or more helpful. Thanks to Mr. Milch and Mr. Addison Metcalf, we are able to reproduce several photographs of Metcalf and related documents. Mr. William Kozlowski, the University of Massachusetts, Class of 1977, has assisted me at every stage of the exhibition, and was especially helpful in the early research and preparation of the catalogue. It was a pleasure to have the counsel of Mr. Richard Mühlberger, Director of the Museum of Fine Arts, Springfield, and the help of Mrs. Gerri Lockwood, Miss Lucille Parent, Mrs. Pauline Reynolds, and Mr. Erick Blaha, all of the Museum of Fine Arts. Mr. Emil Schnorr, conservator, prepared a number of paintings in this exhibition before they were photographed and did so in the midst of a very hectic schedule at the George Walter Vincent Smith Museum. My colleague Mr. Dean Flower read the manuscript with his usual care. Mrs. Henriette Metcalf, of Newtown, Connecticut, granted me the privilege of a memorable interview and has been indispensable to Mrs. de Veer in her research. To them all, and to Mr. William Glick of The Meriden Gravure Company, my sincere thanks.

Francis Murphy, *Guest Curator*

Smith College   Museum of Fine Arts
Northampton,   Springfield, Massachusetts
Massachusetts

WILLARD LEROY METCALF

(1858–1925)

THERE ARE a number of facts about the earliest years of Willard Metcalf's life of which we are uncertain, but we know that he was born in Lowell, Massachusetts, in 1858 and that after his father Greenleaf Metcalf was discharged from the Union forces in 1863, a family farm in Maine served as their home for the next eight years. The family eventually returned to Massachusetts, buying, according to the Cambridge Historical Society, a home at 1 Allston Court, Cambridgeport, in 1872. We know also that Willard worked for a short time in a wholesale hardware store in Boston.

Both of his parents believed in the occult and communicated frequently with "the other side." There seems to be some confusion about just who spoke—Caravaggio or Correggio—but his mother was informed by a medium that Willard would become a famous painter when "the snow of winter lay upon his brow." They decided to encourage their son's gift as best they could. The steps taken by these mildly queer and loving parents were halting but practical: first they arranged an apprenticeship to a wood engraver, then to the painter George Loring Brown. Simultaneously he took life classes at Lowell Institute two evenings a week. Willard walked from Cambridge to Brown's South Boston studio every day: six miles each way. His father, a violinist with the Boston Orchestra, paid Brown faithfully, but with increasing reluctance when the artist swore at his pupil and threw brushes at him. But the young man had unquestionably improved as a draughtsman and the example of Brown's success was not lost on them.

In April of 1876 Willard took leave of this impatient master who had relentlessly required him to labor over a large canvas Willard refers to in his diary (now available through the Archives of American Art) as "that darned old Rome." The classical iconography—scales of Justice and brows crowned with laurel—was to be left behind, although twenty years later these old clichés were dusted off when he entered a contest for circuit court murals and, by invitation in 1898–1899 painted murals for the United States Appellate Court at Madison Square in New York.

In the summer of 1876 Metcalf and Brown called a truce and they met on amiable terms in the White Mountains of New Hampshire where they sketched together. Willard sold small paintings—probably not unlike those of 1874 and 1877 included in this exhibition—to boardinghouse guests and expected to make his own way when the summer was over.

As it happened, however, he received the first scholarship given by the newly formed Museum of Fine Arts School in Boston. He always distinguished between drawing from nature and drawing in the studio. It was his custom to inscribe, with pride, on the reverse of his canvases, "done from nature at Killington Peak" or "done from nature at Artist's Brook."

At an early age he became a fine naturalist. He had the innate ability to assemble, analyse and annotate. He explored the meadows and woods with patience and he pursued his objectives with integrity. He cared about accuracy. His carefully boxed collections of birds' eggs and nests are inscribed and dated. They inform us not only where we too might find the Savanna sparrow, but also that the artist was in Walpole, Maine, in 1905 or in Giverny, France, on May 27, 1888. His sketchbooks tell us that he was in Grez and Giverny in early 1884; his note-taking as a naturalist tells us that he was in Fourges in May and June of 1885.

In 1881, however, Metcalf was still studying art and collecting eggs and nests on this side of the Atlantic. He was twenty-three and impatient to try something new. "Failing health" seemed to necessitate a change. In April he headed for New Mexico and the Zuni. None of the surviving sketches suggest any lack of vigor on Metcalf's part. An Army engineer who met him in the company of a Mr. Sylvester Baxter of the *Boston Herald* was impressed with them both and made note of Metcalf's portfolio of "very successful sketches." The following spring Metcalf's first work for popular magazines appeared in *Harper's*. Baxter wrote "The Father of the Pueblos" and Metcalf provided illustrations. At about the same time that Baxter and Metcalf appeared in *Harper's*, Frank Cushing, the Smithsonian's first ethnologist-anthropologist, published an article in the *Atlantic Monthly* on his explorations of the Grand Canyon. In order to penetrate the deepest mysteries of the Zunis, and to be admitted to the Order of the Ka-Ka, the most sacred of all Zuni orders, Cushing escorted several Zunis to the Atlantic Ocean and to the White House where he was received in Washington by President Arthur. As a consequence, both Baxter and Metcalf made the trip back East early in 1882 and recorded, in their separate ways, the journey of six Zunis to Deer Island in Boston Harbor. Metcalf's old friends in the Paint and Clay Club flocked around to stare and sketch, and scholars at Wellesley and Harvard were quite interested.

Metcalf returned to the Zuni, Baxter did not. In 1889, Cushing, very ill, pointed with pride to a reproduction of *The Arab Market* on the wall of his hospital room. This was Metcalf's painting that had been given honorable mention at the Paris Salon the year before, and Cushing's visitor made note of his pleasure in the success of his fondly remembered comrade. The notes of the Secretary of the Smithsonian Institution for his annual report for 1883 read: "On the first day of May Cushing set out, accompanied by his artist friend W. L. Metcalf and two Indians. His discoveries near the Escudilla, and further north in Eastern Arizona, were his most important."

As for the Indians themselves, they thought highly enough of Metcalf to initiate him into one of their orders, for he signed one of his paintings with his totem as well as his name.

He also acted as scribe for Chief Pa-lo-wah-ti-wa in conveying his thanks to President Arthur for his executive order of May 1, 1883, guaranteeing the Zunis their ownership of Nutria Springs, which General Logan and his relatives had tried to preempt. The letter is a deeply moving document. Cushing's second publishing venture, a three-part essay, "My Adventures in Zuni," was published in *Century Magazine*, and this time he had the Smithsonian's approval. It was illustrated by Henry Farny and Willard Metcalf; Metcalf's were drawn "from nature." Another collaboration with Sylvester Baxter appeared in 1885, but the idea for "Along the Rio Grande" was fully developed, even to its title, in 1882.

In 1876 the time seemed right for a number of American artists to leave for France and Germany. The years 1883–1884 turned out to be another period for fruitful exile. Metcalf determined to see Europe. He had had enough of Arizona's stunted pine and sagebrush. He was tired of getting his six-foot-four frame into six-and-a-half-foot-high pueblos. He had enough money from the magazines and from an exhibition of seventy-five paintings, held in Boston at Chase's Galleries the previous March, and last-minute sales made on the verandahs of affluent shorefront hotels just before he boarded ship. Once he had made up his mind he moved quickly: Arizona in May, Chicago in mid-June, Bisham-on-the-Thames on July fifth. His parents heard from him twice in the next six years. He walked and sketched the summer away in England until it was time to go to Paris in October and draw for Boulanger and Lefebvre.

Life in Paris agreed with him. It gave him confidence. He studied at Julian's all winter, but got back to England in the spring of '84, then recrossed the Channel to Pont Aven in Brittany and eventually wandered to Grez and Giverny (knives and forks chained to the table at his pension) to fill out a perfect summer and fall. The sketches in Brittany show a loosening up, a pleasing, scribbling, elbow-moving freedom. He had spent a good part of the previous winter on *A Bacchanalian Scene*, a carefully painted orgy, which must have made him wonder if he was ever to be rid of George Loring Brown, and yet seemed appropriate to his present life.

During the next years, 1885–1886, he seems to have been pursuing art more at Grez and Giverny than attending class at the Julian Academy. In the summer of '85 Renoir, Cezanne, and, of course, Monet were at Giverny, but Whistler and Degas were painting at Dieppe. Metcalf knew very well that he and Whistler shared the same birthplace, and a natural curiosity might have prompted him to try for a look at his controversial countryman. He wrote a friend in March that he would leave the next day, having just sold two paintings, to find a place just north of Dieppe where he, Ritter, Robinson, Wendel, and others could stay for the summer. Whether or not he did, a sprinkling of "Nocturnes" and "Studies in Purple, White, and Gold" eventually surfaced, and—somewhat more mystifying—some of Twachtman's studies at Arques-la-Bataille that summer bear a striking similarity to Metcalf's at Grez in Chadwick's garden. He also managed to paint a number of pictures at Walberswick on the coast of Suffolk, and return once again to Giverny and Grez.

One of Willard's teachers, Lefebvre, made excellent drawings of camels. He had a drawer full of drawings, and his drawings of camels were usually the first to be pulled out when he wished to make a point in teaching or during an interview. Metcalf left in the fall of 1887 for Tunis and Morocco, and his camels came to equal his teacher's. In 1888, as noted, he won an honorable mention at the Salon for his *Arab Market*. The next year he packed up and returned home, fully expecting word of his recently acquired award to have preceded him. His old editor at Scribner's, however, merely looked up at him blankly and said, "Where have *you* been?"—then handed him an assignment of designing a majuscule, for which he paid him $2.00.

The west fifties, with the Sixth Avenue El, meat markets, stables, and "quick lunch" signs were the home of the avant garde; the "old school" artists stayed downtown. Metcalf moved uneasily between these two worlds for years, as if trying to find a compromise between them that would satisfy his need to make a living and determine once and for all what *his* art would be. He lived uptown in the neighborhood of the Sherwood Studio Building, but taught on 23rd at the Art Students League for a year, then at Cooper Institute for ten years, taking over Will Low's job as instructor of the women's antique classes. Close friends were Hassam, Weir, the architect Charles Platt, and Stanford White. Then in 1896 he and Hassam exchanged milieus—just by chance—Hassam going uptown to the fifties, Metcalf taking up residence with Robert Reid, with whom he was frequently confused on account of their hirsute heads and tall stature, at the Studio Building on West Tenth Street. He was working hard at illustration, doing well, painting when he could—in fact, winning occasional medals at exhibitions—and building up a life-long contempt of female artists.

At the age of forty-three (1901), he married a very young and pretty girl from New Orleans, Marguerite Beaufort Haile. She had modelled for him for some time, but the marriage did not compensate for many things that were going sour for him at the turn of the century. He had been the first to sign, with a bravura flourish, The Ten's agreement to secede from the Society of American Artists and to exhibit thereafter together. But his notices were disheartening. On March 14, 1898, soon after The Ten's first show at Durand-Ruel Gallery, he was dropped from the Players Club—to be reinstated a month later, however—but it was a time of troubles. His murals at the Appellate Court on Madison Square were well done, but he could hardly have enjoyed the work. And Twachtman, whom he dearly loved, died, alone, in Gloucester in 1902. It was time to reexamine his own goals. After classes at Cooper terminated in May of 1903, he left for Maine to live with his parents, while Marguerite enjoyed some sort of career in the theater. A story persists that she was a "Florodora" girl. Certainly she was not one of the original sextet, all of whom married millionaires.

That year he and his mother went out in a flatboat fishing day after day, for they lived on the catch. His father's income was eight and a half dollars a month, his Civil War veteran's pension. There were times, of course, when their son left

Clark's Cove and tented alone by the Damariscotta where he at last was painting what he knew he wanted to paint—not people, not hats nor shoes nor markets nor camels, but the water, earth, and trees of New England. He gave up drinking for a time.

His first personal exhibition was held at the Fishel, Adler, and Schwartz Gallery in February, 1904, and Royal Cortissoz, long an admirer, praised all twenty-one paintings as evidence of his "new" approach. Several of the works in the exhibition, however, including fine paintings from the '90's, had been brought out of storage.

"A partial history of the Renaissance," Metcalf wrote on the first page of the scrapbook he began to keep. But it took two years, really, for the public to become aware of his renaissance. A second exhibition the following year was well received but still not remunerative. He was compelled to return to teaching, instructing night classes at the Rhode Island School of Design, commuting from New York twice a week. With the third year success came, but in Boston, not New York, where his exhibition at the St. Botolphe Club was a virtually complete sellout.

Albert Milch helped make the difference in 1906. He was very young—not the "life-long friend" that persists in stories about Metcalf and Milch. Born in Budapest in 1880, he was still in his twenties, trained as a gilder and framer, when he crossed paths with Metcalf. He framed all the new paintings on credit, accompanied him to Boston, and provided the management and encouragement needed by the nervous art-

ist. He was to play the same role of both friend and agent to an expanding circle of artists, including Julian Alden Weir, Childe Hassam, J. Francis Murphy, Bruce Crane, and many others.

Milch, seeing his friend safely reassured by both prestige and remuneration, returned to New York, only to be called back by Metcalf's friends to rescue him from a binge of several days. Casting about in his mind for some appropriately solemn or sacred place, yet knowing the artist was not a church-going man, Milch pulled, pushed, or guided the artist as far as the steps of a sanctuary and, on the threat of severing their relationship if he did not comply, exacted from him a promise not to drink again.

It is not usual in the ordinary course of things for friendship to outlast a break in a shared way of living. Metcalf's friend Childe Hassam continued on his high, wide, and handsome way, while Metcalf accepted the path of plainer living. Still, they remained close, Hassam among the few persons able to jolly his friend into laughter and relaxation. He enticed him to Old Lyme where Metcalf, in turn, lured others. His continuing success and his award of the first Corcoran gold medal and Clarke prize for *May Night*, a painting of Miss Florence Griswold's home in Lyme under the enchantment of moonlight, convinced innumerable other artists that they, too, could succeed by painting and learning in so happy an environment. Metcalf's dissatisfaction with Old Lyme seems to have been precipitated not only by the touch of fame but by his young wife running off with Robert Nisbet, one of his students. Metcalf, although suffering some embarrassment, was not overwhelmed by the event.

What is surprising is how quickly Metcalf plunged into a second marriage upon his divorce from Marguerite. His new bride, Henriette McCrea, was not only almost thirty years younger than he, but a person who, by temperament, lived comfortably with extremes: an active dedication to humane services and a youthful zest for meeting and mixing with the interesting people of her day, particularly those in the theatre. When they met, however, it was her odd and inviting beauty, her worldly command of French, Italian, and German, and the contrasting innocence of her convent-bred attitudes that amused, stimulated, and swept Metcalf off his feet. They had two children, Rosalind and Addison, and many comfortable years together. But the marriage could not possibly have ended in any way other than divorce. The marvel of it is that it lasted ten years. The artist had long established for himself a routine that no woman could basically alter.

When at home, he left the apartment each morning at eight, dressed in a business suit, on his way for the day to his studio apartment at des Artistes. His son recalls the delicately constructed fly, one of many beauties made in leisure moments for trout fishing, tucked into his hatband. Upon his return in the evening, he dined, then as often as not went to a movie down at the corner, murder mysteries being a favorite. He adored his children, but kept his distance. He seldom went anywhere with Henriette socially, but at least once, perhaps several times, went to Hamlin Garland's for seances. Trips to such places as Henryville, Pennsylvania, and Newfoundland, fishing for trout and salmon, were ritual events at least once and sometimes twice a year. He had shifted from the Players Club to the Century and was a Coffee House habitué. Booth Tarkington and he became close friends.

He was now acclaimed as "the poet laureate" of the New

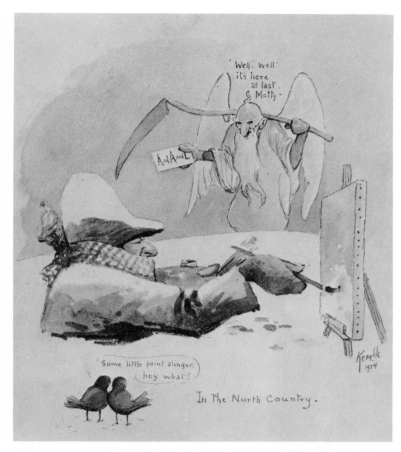

In the North Country, by E. W. Kimble. Courtesy of Mr. Harold C. Milch.

England hills. There were honors and more honors, purchases and more purchases. The highly selective Charles Freer bought four paintings for his new gallery at the Smithsonian. Throughout the country there were few museums that did not respond to the special quality of his canvases by buying at least one of them. His manner became that of the teaching master. He no longer offered opinions—he delivered them. So reports his frequent visitor, Marcus Goodrich, who had been hand-picked by Metcalf to succeed him as husband to Henriette and second father to his children.

Unlike some of his colleagues, Metcalf refused membership in the National Academy. Only months before he died, however, he was elected to the American Academy of Arts and Letters. E. W. Kemble's cartoon was drawn for a dinner to honor this occasion. Nothing else remains of that event, but if Metcalf spoke at all about his aim as an artist he probably would have echoed sentiments expressed to his daughter Rosalind when she was fourteen: "One has thoughts for hardly anything but the making of . . . [and] the endless effort of putting paint on a canvas—with a miserable little brush— and endeavoring to make it express thoughts and dreams that will perhaps reach out and say something to someone, something that will make wandering souls stop and look, perhaps waken something in them that may make them think of beautiful things, and so perhaps [enjoy] happiness." It is hard to argue with Metcalf's aspirations and the beautiful examples found in this exhibition prove how often he realized them.

Elizabeth de Veer

January 1, 1976
Englewood, New Jersey

CATALOGUE

The Ten, 1903, on the occasion of William Merritt Chase replacing John Henry Twachtman. Seated, left to right, Edward Simmons, Willard Metcalf, Childe Hassam, J. Alden Weir, and Robert Reid. Standing, left to right, William Merritt Chase, Frank W. Benson, Edmund V. Tarbell, Thomas W. Dewing, and Joseph R. DeCamp. The photograph was signed by the group and presented to Albert Milch as a gesture of their friendship. Courtesy of Mr. Harold C. Milch.

1. *RIVER LANDSCAPE*
Oil on canvas, $9^3/_4'' \times 14^5/_8''$
Signed l.l. and dated 1874
Lent by Corcoran Gallery of Art, Gift of Estelle Cheffield
Bechhoefer, 1965 (65.29)

2. *LITTLE EDDIE*
Oil on canvas, $16'' \times 10''$
Signed and titled on back
Lent by Pierce Galleries, Inc.
In Metcalf's diary he notes that a little girl named Edna, possibly his sister, died in 1876, at age seven and a half.

3. *SANDY HOLLOW, MANCHESTER, MASSACHUSETTS*
Oil on canvas, $11^1/_2'' \times 17^1/_2''$
Signed l.r. and dated 1877
Lent by Vose Galleries of Boston, Incorporated, Boston, Massachusetts
Metcalf's sketchbook (Archives of American Art) includes drawings executed at Manchester in 1877.

4. *DIAMOND ISLAND, CASCO BAY, MAINE*
Oil on canvas, $14'' \times 18''$
Signed l.r. and dated 1879
Lent by Smith College Museum of Art, Gift of Mrs. Edward G. Gallagher (Margaret Richardson '06)

5. *GIRL AT THE PIANO*
Oil on wood, $15^1/_4'' \times 18^1/_4''$
Signed l.l.
Lent by Hirschl and Adler Galleries, Inc.

6. *TURKEYS IN A FIELD*
Oil on canvas, $12^1/_2'' \times 18''$
Signed l.r.
Lent anonymously
Shown at the Museum of Fine Arts, Springfield, only.

7. *UNTITLED LANDSCAPE*
Oil on board, $8^1/_4'' \times 13^3/_4''$
Signed l.r. and dated 1887
Lent by Dr. Sellers J. Thomas, Jr.

8. *TEN CENT BREAKFAST*
Oil on canvas, $15'' \times 22''$
Signed l.r. and dated Giverny, 1887
Lent by The Denver Art Museum, The Edward and Tullah Hanley Memorial Gift for the People of Denver and the Area (A-1504)
Shown at The Munson-Williams-Proctor Institute, Utica, and the Museum of Fine Arts, Springfield, only.
Seated at the table left to right are John Henry Twachtman, Theodore Robinson, and Robert Louis Stevenson. There is some question about the standing figure, but Reginald Birch or Lowell Birge Harrison are most frequently mentioned. Given what is known about Stevenson's itinerary the place and date present a problem.

9. *STREET SCENE, TUNIS*
Oil on fabric, $14^{15}/_{16}'' \times 9^3/_4''$
Signed l.l. and dated Tunis, 1887
Lent by Worcester Art Museum, Bequest of Grenville H.
Norcross, 1937 (1937.42)
A study for number 10.

10. *STREET SCENE, TUNIS*
Oil on canvas, $32^1/_2'' \times 21^1/_2''$
Signed l.l. and dated 1887
Lent by Berry-Hill Galleries

11. *SUNLIGHT AND SHADOW*
Oil on canvas, $12^3/_4'' \times 16^1/_8''$
Signed l.l. and dated 1888
Lent by The Museum of Fine Arts, Houston, Gift of Miss Ima
Hogg (41-28)

12. *VILLAGE STREET SCENE*
Oil on canvas, $12^3/_4'' \times 18^1/_2''$
Signed l.l. and dated 1888
Lent by Mr. Scott L. Probasco, Jr.

13. *SUMMER TWILIGHT*
Oil on canvas, $34^1/_4'' \times 35''$
Signed l.l. and dated 1890
Lent by Mr. and Mrs. Fred D. Bentley, Sr., and Mr. and Mrs.
J. Alan Sellars

14. *BY THE RIVER (THE DOMAIN, SYDNEY)*
Gouache, $18^3/_4'' \times 25^3/_8''$
Signed l.r.
Lent by Hirschl and Adler Galleries, Inc.
Robert Louis Stevenson's *The Wrecker*, written in collaboration with Lloyd Osbourne, was published serially in 1891–

1892. Metcalf illustrated the New York edition published by Charles Scribner's Sons in 1892. The full caption for this illustration is: "The Domain, Sydney. My word, no! replied the little man. I just sit here and read the *Dead Bird*." The *Dead Bird* is a newspaper and the Domain is a park in Sydney, Australia. The early chapters are set in Paris and are concerned with the life of an American art student identified as Will H. Low.

15. *NORTH WEST PACIFIC COAST LODGE UNDER CONSTRUCTION*
Gouache, $9'' \times 10^1/_2''$
Unsigned
Lent by Kennedy Galleries, Inc.

16. *GLOUCESTER HARBOR*
Oil on canvas, $26'' \times 28^3/_4''$
Signed l.l. and dated 1895
Lent by Mead Art Gallery, Amherst College, Gift of Mr. George
D. Pratt, 1932 (P1932.16)
Shown at the Museum of Fine Arts, Springfield, and The Currier Gallery of Art, only.

17. *SAVANNA SPARROW*
Watercolor with pen and ink on cardboard, $9'' \times 7^1/_2''$
Signed l.r. and dated Walpole, Maine, June 7, 1904
Lent by Mr. and Mrs. Paul Feltman

18. *AFTERNOON BREEZE*
Oil on canvas, $29'' \times 26''$
Signed l.l. and dated 1904
Lent by Mrs. F. Bailey Hall

19. *THE LOG HOUSE*
Oil on canvas, 29″ × 26″
Signed l.r.
Lent by Mr. and Mrs. Patrick Wilmerding

20. *MAY NIGHT*
Oil on canvas, 39 1/2″ × 36 3/8″
Signed l.l. and dated 1906
Lent by Corcoran Gallery of Art, Purchased by Gallery Fund, 1907 (07.7)
The Greek Revival house in the painting belonged to Miss Florence Griswold in Old Lyme, Connecticut, where Metcalf was an active member of the artists' colony.

21. *FIRST SNOW*
Oil on canvas, 25 3/4″ × 28 3/4″
Signed l.r. and dated 1906
Lent by the Museum of Fine Arts, Boston, Bequest of Ernest Wadsworth Longfellow (23.483)

22. *SUMMER*
Pastel, 9″ × 12″
Signed l.l. and dated 1906
Lent by Mrs. F. Bailey Hall

23. *HILLSIDE*
Pastel, 9″ × 12″
Signed l.l. and dated 1906
Lent by Mrs. F. Bailey Hall

24. *TREE* (not illustrated)
Pencil and chalk drawing, 11 5/8″ × 13 3/5″
Signed l.l. and dated 1907
Lent by Mead Art Gallery, Amherst College, Gift of Elizabeth Ball (1955.310)

25. *THE BOWER*
Oil on canvas, 26″ × 29″
Signed l.r. and dated 1907
Lent by Mr. and Mrs. Justin D. Miller
Formerly in the collection of William T. Evans.

26. *TROUT BROOK*
Oil on canvas, 26″ × 29″
Signed l.r. and dated 1907
Lent by The Currier Gallery of Art, Manchester, New Hampshire

27. *MAY PASTORAL*
Oil on canvas, 36 1/4″ × 39″
Signed l.l. and dated 1907
Lent by the Museum of Fine Arts, Boston, Charles Henry Hayden Fund (08.325)

28. *INDIAN SUMMER*
Oil on canvas, 26″ × 29″
Signed l.l. and dated 1908
Lent by Mrs. F. Bailey Hall

29. *OCTOBER*
Oil on canvas, 26″ × 29″
Signed l.l. and dated 1908
Lent by the Heirs of Mr. Frederick Harris
Painted at Leete's Island, Connecticut.

30. *MAYTIME*
    Oil on canvas, 26″ × 29″
    Signed l.l. and dated 1914
    Lent by the Akron Art Institute, the Edwin C. Shaw Collection
    Although dated 1914, a letter from Metcalf to Thomas W.
    Dunbar dated March 15, 1917, states that "it was painted at
    Leete's Island, Connecticut, in the spring of 1909."

31. *ICEBOUND*
    Oil on canvas, 29″ × 26⅛″
    Signed l.l. and dated 1909
    Lent by The Art Institute of Chicago, Walter H. Schulze Memorial Collection (1910.311)

32. *THE HUSH OF WINTER*
    Oil on canvas, 25½″ × 28½″
    Signed l.l. and dated 1911
    Lent by Mr. and Mrs. Justin D. Miller
    Painted in Cornish, New Hampshire.

33. *WILLOWS IN MARCH*
    Oil on canvas, 26″ × 29″
    Signed l.l.
    Lent by Smith College Museum of Art, Gift of Mrs. Charles W.
    Carl (Marie Schuster '17)
    Painted in Cornish, New Hampshire, 1911, as recorded in
    Metcalf's Cash Book.

34. *EARLY SPRING AFTERNOON—CENTRAL PARK*
    Oil on canvas, 36″ × 36⅛″
    Signed l.l. and dated 1911
    Lent by The Brooklyn Museum, Brooklyn, Frank L. Babbott
    Fund (66.85)
    According to Mrs. Henriette Metcalf, this painting was executed in the Metcalf's New York apartment at Central Park
    West.

35. *FALLING SNOW*
    Oil on canvas, 26½″ × 29″
    Signed l.r. and dated 1913
    Lent by the Museum of Fine Arts, Springfield, Massachusetts,
    The Horace P. Wright Collection
    Painted in Cornish, New Hampshire.

36. *PONT ROYAL*
    Oil on canvas, 31½″ × 34½″
    Signed l.l. and dated Paris, 1913
    Lent by Chapellier Galleries, Inc.
    Exhibited "The Ten," 1914; formerly in the collection of The
    High Museum of Art, Atlanta, Georgia, under the title *Pont
    Neuf.*

37. *OLD MILL, PELAGO, ITALY*
    Oil on canvas, 26″ × 29″
    Signed l.l.
    Lent by Davis and Long Company
    Painted in 1913.

38. *PELAGO—TUSCANY*
    Oil on canvas, 26¼″ × 29″
    Signed l.l. and dated 1913
    Lent by the Albright-Knox Art Gallery, Buffalo, New York,
    Sherman S. Jewett Fund, 1917

39. *OLD HOMESTEAD, CONNECTICUT*
    Oil on canvas, 26″ × 29″
    Signed l.r.
    Lent by The St. Louis Art Museum, Museum Purchase (253.15)
    Painted in 1914

40. *NUT GATHERING*
Oil on canvas, $24\frac{1}{2}'' \times 24\frac{1}{2}''$
Signed l.l.
Lent by the Munson-Williams-Proctor Institute, Utica, Gift through the Charles E. Merrill Trust (73.160)

41. *DRAWINGS*
Pencil and chalk, $25\frac{1}{4}'' \times 19\frac{3}{4}''$
Initialed l.r.
Lent by the Mead Art Gallery, Amherst College, Gift of The Milch Gallery, 1933 (D 1933.20)

42. *FEMALE NUDE*
Pencil and chalk, $25'' \times 19\frac{1}{4}''$
Initialed l.r.
Lent by the Mead Art Gallery, Amherst College, Gift of The Milch Gallery, 1933 (D 1933.16)

43. *MALE NUDE*
Pencil and chalk, $24\frac{1}{2}'' \times 18\frac{3}{4}''$
Initialed l.r.
Lent by the Mead Art Gallery, Amherst College, Gift of The Milch Gallery, 1933 (D 1933.17)

44. *VILLAGE IN LATE SPRING*
Oil on canvas, $29\frac{1}{2}'' \times 33\frac{1}{4}''$
Signed l.r. and dated 1920
Lent by Mr. and Mrs. Carl Navarre
Painted in Woodbury, Connecticut.
Shown at the Hunter Museum of Art, Chattanooga, only.

45. *SPRING IN THE VALLEY*
Oil on canvas, $25\frac{1}{2}'' \times 28\frac{1}{4}''$
Signed l.r.
Lent by Coe Kerr Gallery, Inc.
Painted in Chester, Vermont, 1921.

46. *MARCH THAW*
Oil on canvas, $38'' \times 39''$
Signed l.l. and dated 1922
Lent by Mr. and Mrs. Salim L. Lewis
Painted in Chester, Vermont.

47. *INDIAN SUMMER, VERMONT*
Oil on canvas, $50\frac{1}{4}'' \times 60\frac{1}{8}''$
Signed l.l. and dated 1922
Lent by the Dallas Museum of Fine Arts, Dallas, Texas (1973.83)
Painted in Chester, Vermont. Metcalf is known to have painted a smaller version of this work.

48. *NOVEMBER MOSAIC*
Oil on canvas, $26'' \times 28''$
Signed l.l. and dated 1922
Lent by The New Britain Museum of American Art, John Butler Talcott Fund (1925.1)
Painted in Chester, Vermont.

49. *NOVEMBER*
Oil on canvas, $39\frac{1}{2}'' \times 36\frac{1}{4}''$
Signed l.l. and dated 1922
Lent by Mr. and Mrs. Colin M. Curtis
This painting portrays the Little Williams River, Chester, Vermont.

50. *IN THE NORTH COUNTRY*
Oil on canvas, 39$^7/_8$" × 45"
Signed l.l. and dated 1923
Lent by The Metropolitan Museum of Art, Purchased,
George A. Hearn Fund, 1924 (24.60)
Shown at the Museum of Fine Arts, Springfield, only.

51. *MELTING SNOWS*
Oil on board, 7$^1/_2$" × 9$^1/_4$"
Signed l.l., estate seal on back
Lent anonymously
According to Metcalf's Cash Book this painting was sold as
Winter on March 27, 1925, by The Milch Gallery, eighteen
days after Metcalf's death on March 9.

ILLUSTRATIONS

. RIVER LANDSCAPE   1874

2. LITTLE EDDIE c. 1876

5. AT THE PIANO c. 1880

3. SANDY HOLLOW, MANCHESTER, MASSACHUSETTS 1877

4. DIAMOND ISLAND, CASCO BAY, MAINE   1879

6. TURKEYS IN A FIELD   C. 1886

7. UNTITLED LANDSCAPE 1887

9. STREET SCENE, TUNIS   1887

10. STREET SCENE, TUNIS   1887

8. TEN CENT BREAKFAST   1887

11. SUNLIGHT AND SHADOW   1888

12. VILLAGE STREET SCENE 1888

13. SUMMER TWILIGHT 1890

14. BY THE RIVER (THE DOMAIN, SYDNEY) C. 1892

15. NORTHWEST PACIFIC COAST LODGE UNDER CONSTRUCTION   C. 1892

16. GLOUCESTER HARBOR 1895

No. 542 a   AMMODRAMVS   SANDWICHENSIS   SAVANNA ♀   Wilson

Savanna Sparrow   ♂

Length 5.43   Wings extended 8.13   Length of Wing 2.62   Tail 1.95.   Bill .40

Length of Claws 1.   Tarsus .77   Middle toe .61

1st 3 primaries same length.   18 outer primaries and secondaries

2nd and 3rd primaries   Tail - 5 feathers on each side

outer 2. same length

inner 2. sharply pointed

Range, Eastern North America ; breeds from Missouri and northern New Jersey, north to
        Labrador and Hudsons Bay ; and winters from southern Illinois and Virginia,
        southward to Cuba and Mexico.

Nest, on the ground, in open field, under tussock of grass, carefully concealed, the brim of
        nest being flush with the ground, and loosely constructed, composed externally of
        coarse grasses and moss, and lined with finer grasses, measuring, external diameter
        4.25 by 2.50 in height; the cavity is 2.25 diam. by 1.60 deep.

Eggs, five, bluish white ground color, heavily marked at larger end with reddish brown and
        cinnamon with some lavender, obscuring ground color, and forming ring around the large
        end. —   measuring   1. — .71 × .56   taken June 7. 1904 incubation five

2. — .74 × .59   days advanced. — Walpole Maine

3. — .73 × .58

4. — .77 × .57   Willard L. Kelsey

5. — .73 × .59

18. AFTERNOON BREEZE   1904

19. THE LOG HOUSE   C. 1905

20. MAY NIGHT 1906

W.L. METCALF. 1907

25. THE BOWER 1907

W.L.METCALF. '06

22. SUMMER   1906

23. HILLSIDE 1906

21. FIRST SNOW   1906

26. TROUT BROOK 1907

27. MAY PASTORAL   1907

28. INDIAN SUMMER 1908

29. OCTOBER 1908

30. MAYTIME 1914 (painted 1909)

31. ICEBOUND 1909

32. THE HUSH OF WINTER 1911

33. WILLOWS IN MARCH 1911

35. FALLING SNOW   1913

36. PONT ROYAL   1913

34. EARLY SPRING AFTERNOON, CENTRAL PARK   1911

37. OLD MILL, PELAGO, ITALY   1913

38. PELAGO—TUSCANY   1913

39. OLD HOMESTEAD, CONNECTICUT   1914

40. NUT GATHERING   C. 1915

41. DRAWINGS

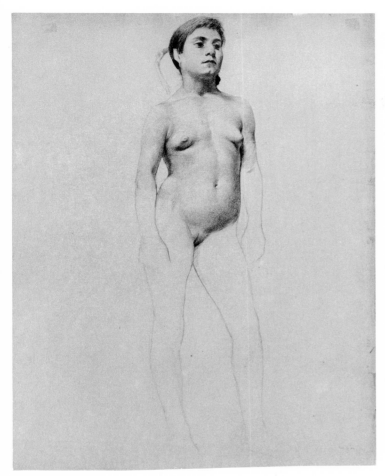

42. FEMALE NUDE

43. MALE NUDE

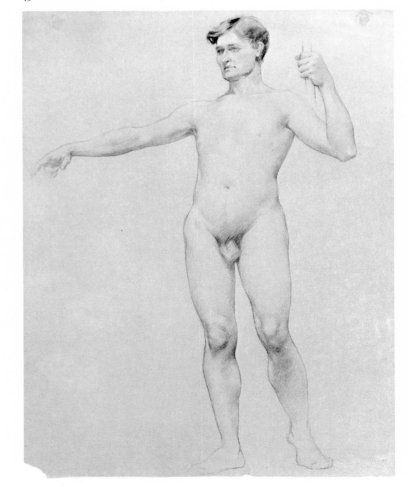

44. VILLAGE IN LATE SPRING   1920

45. SPRING IN THE VALLEY   1921

46. MARCH THAW   1922

47. INDIAN SUMMER, VERMONT   1922

48. NOVEMBER MOSAIC 1922

50. IN THE NORTH COUNTRY   1923

51. MELTING SNOWS

Produced in an edition of 1500 copies for
the Museum of Fine Arts, Springfield,
by The Stinehour Press, Lunenburg, Vermont,
and
The Meriden Gravure Company,
Meriden, Connecticut